# Quick Inspirations

## Inspiring millions of people each and every day!

**THE WORLD'S MOST SHARED INSPIRATIONS**
**QuickInspirations.com**

bonus books

Chicago and Los Angeles

06   05   04   03   02                    5   4   3   2   1

Library of Congress Control Number: 2002108387
ISBN: 1-56625-187-7

Bonus Books
160 East Illinois Street
Chicago, Illinois 60611


Printed in the United States of America

**RAJNIKANT V. BECHAR**
"Gayatri Nivas"
6, Sherrard Road
Forest Gate
London E7 8DW UK
Tel.: 0208 - 4713715
rvbechar@googlemail.com

Inspiring millions of people
each and every day!

# Table of Contents

# Foreword

With this, our first edition of *Quick Inspirations*, our sincerest thanks go out to the subscribers who have so thoughtfully sent us the content which composes it, and to the authors and publishers who have generously permitted us to reprint their inspirational words.

As much of the material comes to us without authorship, it has been a pleasurable task to find and credit writers before presenting their work. We regret, however, that in some cases, our search has failed to discover their names and we had to print some articles as "unknown." Should this book fall into the hands of some author to whom credit is not given, we would deem it a favor to hear from you.

We hope that *Quick Inspirations*, made possible by our subscribers, publishers, and some of the world's greatest writers, will fall into appreciative hands and that their generosity will be repaid in knowing that many human hearts and lives have been touched as a result of their good thoughts and deeds.

The Staff of Quick Inspirations

# Attitude and Outlook

$W$hether you think you can or think you can't—you are right.

*Henry Ford*

*N*o one can make you feel inferior without your consent.

*Eleanor Roosevelt*

When you come to the edge of all the
    light you know,
and are about to step off into the dark-
    ness of the unknown,
faith is knowing one of two things will
    happen:
There will be something solid to stand on,
or you will be taught how to fly.

*Barbara J. Winter*

$O$ut of clutter, find Simplicity.
From discord, find Harmony.
In the middle of difficulty lies Opportunity.

*Albert Einstein*

*I*f I had my life to live over: I'd like to make more mistakes next time. I'd relax . . . I would start barefoot earlier in the spring and stay that way later in the fall. I would ride more merry-go-rounds. I would pick more daisies.

*Nadine Stair, Elderly resident of Louisville, Kentucky*

$\boldsymbol{Y}$esterday is history,
tomorrow is a mystery,
and today is a gift;
that's why they call it the present.

*Author Unknown*

*Y*ou are your greatest asset, there is
nothing you can't do.
No one can keep you from dreaming, only
you can stop them coming true.
Your achievements are determined, by
the desire that you possess.
Believe in who you are. Believe in what
you do.
It's not a quirk of fate, it's strictly up to
you.

*Author Unknown*

*P*eople who soar are those who refuse to sit back, sigh and wish things would change. They neither complain of their lot nor passively dream of some distant ship coming in. Rather, they visualize in their minds that they are not quitters; they will not allow life's circumstances to push them down and hold them under.

*Charles R. Swindoll*

# Character

*E*veryone tries to define this thing called character. It's not hard. Character is doing what's right when nobody's looking.

*J. C. Watts*

On Judgement Day, God will not look you over for medals, degrees, or diplomas, but for scars.

*Elbert Hubbard*

*T*he best index to a person's character is how he treats people who can't do him any good, and how he treats people who can't fight back.

*Abigail Van Buren*

*W*hat you possess in the world will be found at the day of your death to belong to someone else. But what you are will be yours forever.

*Henry Van Dyke*

*B*e more concerned with your character than your reputation, because your character is what you really are, while your reputation is merely what others think you are.

*John Wooden*

*D*uring my eighty-seven years I have witnessed a whole succession of technological revolutions. But none of them has done away with the need for character in the individual or the ability to think.

*Bernard Baruch*

*P*eople are unreasonable, illogical, and
    self-centered.
Love them anyway.
If you do good, people may accuse you of
    selfish motives.
Do good anyway.
If you are successful, you may win false
    friends and true enemies.
Succeed anyway.
The good you do today may be forgotten
    tomorrow.
Do good anyway.
Honesty and transparency make you vul-
    nerable.
Be honest and transparent anyway.
What you spend years building may be
    destroyed overnight.
Build anyway.
People who really want help may attack
    you if you help them.
Help them anyway.
Give the world the best you have and you
    may get hurt.
Give the world your best anyway.

*Mother Teresa*

*W*atch your thoughts; they become your
words.

Watch your words; they become your
actions.

Watch your actions; they become your
habits.

Watch your habits; they become character.

Watch your character; it becomes your
destiny.

*Frank Outlaw*

# Enthusiasm

*E*nthusiasm one of the most powerful engines of success. When you do a thing, do it with your might. Put your whole soul into it. Stamp it with your own personality. Be active, be energetic, be enthusiastic and faithful, and you will accomplish your objective. Nothing great was ever achieved without enthusiasm.

*Ralph Waldo Emerson*

*1* am not afraid of tomorrow, for I have seen yesterday and I love today.

*William Allen White*

*I*f you don't think every day is a good day, just try missing one.

*Cavett Robert*

*I* want to be thoroughly used up when I die, for the harder I work the more I live.

*Author Unknown*

We act as though comfort and luxury were the chief requirements of life, when all that we need to make us happy is something to be enthusiastic about.

*Charles Kingsley*

*S*miling is infectious; you catch it like
    the flu,
When someone smiled at me today, I
    started smiling too.
I passed around the corner, and someone
    saw my grin—
When he smiled I realized, I'd passed it
    on to him.
I thought about that smile, then I realized
    its worth,
A single smile, just like mine, could travel
    round the earth.
So, if you feel a smile begin, don't leave it
    undetected—
Let's start an epidemic quick and get the
    world infected!

*Author Unknown*

**D**on't ask yourself what the world needs; ask yourself what makes you come alive. And then go and do that. Because what the world needs is people who have come alive.

*Harold Whitman*

*W*hen you were born, you cried and the world rejoiced. Live your life in such a manner that when you die, the world cries and you rejoice.

*Old Indian Saying*

# Family

*T*he great gift of family life is to be intimately acquainted with people you might never even introduce yourself to, had life not done it for you.

*Kendall Hailey*

*T*he bond that links your true family is not one of blood, but of respect and joy in each other's life.

*Richard Bach*

*A* baby will make love stronger, days shorter, nights longer, bankroll smaller, home happier, clothes shabbier, the past forgotten, and the future worth living for.

*Anonymous*

*I*f I had my child to raise all over again,
I'd build self-esteem first, and the house
later.
I'd finger-paint more, and point the finger
less.
I would do less correcting and more con-
necting.
I'd take my eyes off my watch, and watch
with my eyes.
I'd take more hikes and fly more kites.
I'd stop playing serious, and seriously
play.
I would run through more fields and gaze
at more stars.
I'd do more hugging and less tugging.

*Diane Loomans*

*E*ach day of our lives we make deposits in the memory banks of our children.

*Charles R. Swindoll*

**Y**ou don't really understand human nature unless you know why a child on a merry-go-round will wave at his parents every time around—and why his parents will always wave back.

*William D. Tammeus*

*T*he family you come from isn't as important as the family you're going to have.

*Ring Lardner*

*T*he most important thing a father can do for his children is to love their mother.

*Henry Ward Beecher*

# Friendship

*F*riendship is unnecessary, like philosophy, like art. . . . It has no survival value; rather it is one to those things that give value to survival.

*C. S. Lewis*

$\Upsilon$our friends will know you better in the first minute you meet than your acquaintances will know you in a thousand years.

*Richard Bach*

*A* true friend is someone who thinks that you are a good egg even though he knows that you are slightly cracked.

*Bernard Meltzer*

*T*he glory of friendship is not the out-stretched hand, nor the kindly smile, nor the joy of companionship; it is the spirited inspiration that comes to one when he discovers that someone else believes in him and is willing to trust him.

*Ralph Waldo Emerson*

*O*ne friend in a lifetime is much; two are many; three are hardly possible.

*Henry Adams*

$S$o long as we love we serve;
So long as we are loved by others,
I would almost say that we are indispen-
   sable;
And no one is useless while they have a
   friend.

*Robert Louis Stevenson*

*E*ach friend represents a world in us, a world possible not born until they arrive, and it is only by this meeting that a new world is born.

*Anais Nin*

*I*f you go looking for a friend, you're going to find they're very scarce. If you go out to be a friend, you'll find them everywhere.

*Zig Ziglar*

# Happiness

*I* have learned from experience that the greater part of our happiness or misery depends on our dispositions and not on our circumstances.

*Martha Washington*

*I*t is not easy to find happiness in ourselves, and it is not possible to find it elsewhere.

*Agnes Repplier*

*R*emember that there is no happiness in having or in getting, but only in giving. Reach out. Share. Smile. Hug. Happiness is a perfume you cannot pour on others without getting a few drops on yourself.

*Og Mandino*

*H*appiness . . . is not a destination: it is a manner of traveling. Happiness is not an end in itself. It is a by-product of working, playing, loving, and living.

*Haim Ginott*

*W*e should try never to let our happy frame of mind be disturbed. Whether we are suffering at present or have suffered in the past, there is no reason to be unhappy. If we can remedy it, why be unhappy? And if we cannot, what use is there being depressed about it? That just adds unhappiness and does no good at all.

*Dalai Lama*

*I* believe the nicest and sweetest days are not those on which anything very splendid or wonderful or exciting happens, but just those that bring simple little pleasures, following one another softly, like pearls off a string.

*L. M. Montgomery*

*I*f you smile when no one else is around, you really mean it.

*Andy Rooney*

*H*appiness requires problems . . . we
need problems for the rewards they bring.

*Oscar Herman*

# Hope and Dreams

*O*nly as high as I reach can I grow,
Only as far as I seek can I go,
Only as deep as I look can I see,
Only as much as I dream can I be.

*Karen Ravn*

*T*wenty years from now you will be more disappointed by the things you didn't do than by the ones you did do. So throw off the bowlines. Sail away from the safe harbor. Catch the trade winds in your sails. Explore. Dream. Discover.

*Mark Twain*

*W*here there is an open mind, there will always be a frontier.

*Charles Kettering*

*D*on't wait for your ship to come in—swim out to it.

*Anonymous*

*I*f you can DREAM it, you can DO it.

*Walt Disney*

*I*t is never too late to be what you might have been.

*George Elliot*

No one really knows enough to be a pessimist.

*Norman Cousins*

*W*hen I was a young man, I wanted to change the world. I found it was difficult to change the world, so I tried to change my nation. When I found I couldn't change the nation, I began to focus on my town. I couldn't change the town and as an older man, I tried to change my family. Now, as an old man, I realize the only thing I can change is myself, and suddenly I realize that if long ago I had changed myself, I could have made an impact on my family. My family and I could have made an impact on our town. Their impact could have changed the nation and I could indeed have changed the world.

*Author Unknown*

# Kindness

*I* expect to pass through this life but once. If, therefore, there can be any kindness I can show, or any good thing that I can do to any fellow being, let me do it now as I shall not pass this way again.

*William Penn*

*I*f someone listens, or stretches out a hand, or whispers a kind word of encouragement, or attempts to understand a lonely person, extraordinary things begin to happen.

*Loretta Gierzatlis*

*C*ount no day lost in which you waited your turn, took only your share, and sought advantage over no one.

*Robert Brault*

*W*e make a living by what we get. We make a life by what we give.

*Winston Churchill*

*H*ating people is like burning your own house down to get rid of a rat.

*Harry Emerson Fosdick*

*I*f you want happiness for an hour—take a nap.

If you want happiness for a day—go fishing.

If you want happiness for a month—get married.

If you want happiness for a year—inherit a fortune.

If you want happiness for a lifetime—help someone else.

*Chinese Proverb*

*N*o person was ever honored for what
he received.  Honor has been the reward
for what he gave

*Calvin Coolidge*

*T*hat best portion of a good man's life; his little, nameless, unremembered acts of kindness and love.

*William Wordsworth*

# Leadership

*I*t is a fine thing to have ability, but the ability to discover ability in others is the true test.

*Elbert Hubbard*

*T* here is a great man who makes every man feel small. But the real great man is the man who makes every man feel great.

*G. K. Chesterton*

$\mathbf{Y}$ou can buy a person's time; you can buy their physical presence at a given place; you can even buy a measured number of their skilled muscular motions per hour. But you cannot buy enthusiasm . . . you cannot buy loyalty. You cannot buy the devotion of hearts, minds, or souls. You must earn these.

*Clarence Francis*

*F*latter me, and I may not believe you.
Criticize me, and I may not like you.
Ignore me, and I may not forgive you.
Encourage me, and I may not forget you.

*William Arthur*

*W*e must view young people not as empty bottles to be filled, but as candles to be lit.

*Robert H. Shaffer*

When Thomas Edison was working on improving his first electric light bulb, the story goes, he handed the finished bulb to a younger helper, who nervously carried it upstairs, step by step. At the last possible moment, the boy dropped it, requiring the whole team to work another 24 hours to make a second bulb. When it was finished, Edison looked around, then handed it to the same boy. The gesture probably changed the boy's life. Edison knew that more than a bulb was at stake.

*James D. Newton*

*I*f we work upon marble, it will perish; if we work upon brass, time will efface it . . . but if we work upon immortal minds . . . we engrave on those tablets something which will brighten all eternity.

*Daniel Webster*

$O$nly those who will risk going too far
can possibly find out how far one can go.

*T.S. Elliot*

# Life and Learning

$\mathcal{W}$hat is life?
Life is a gift . . . accept it
Life is an adventure . . . dare it
Life is a mystery . . . unfold it
Life is a game . . . play it
Life is beauty . . . praise it
Life is a puzzle . . . solve it
Life is opportunity . . . take it
Life is sorrowful . . . experience it
Life is a song . . . sing it
Life is a goal . . . achieve it
Life is a mission . . . fulfill it

*David McNally*

Live as if to die tomorrow,
Learn as if to live forever.

*Gandhi*

**M**inds are like parachutes. They only function when they are open.

*Sir James Dewar*

All men should strive to learn before they die what they are running from, and to, and why.

*James Thurber*

We shall not cease from exploration
And the end of all our exploring
Will be to arrive where we started
And know the place for the first time.

*T. S. Eliot*

*H*umans think they are smarter than dolphins because we build cars and buildings and start wars, etc. . . and all that dolphins do is swim in the water, eat fish and play around. Dolphins believe that they are smarter for exactly the same reasons.

*Douglas Adams*

$G$ood judgment comes from experience, and a lotta that comes from bad judgment.

*Cowboy Wisdom*

*W*e teach best what we most need to learn.

*Author Unknown*

# Love and Romance

$\mathcal{L}$ife has taught us that love does not consist in gazing at each other but in looking outward together in the same direction.

*Antoine de Saint-Exupéry*

*H*ow many loved your moments of glad
    grace,
And loved your beauty with love false or
    true;
But one man loved the pilgrim soul in
    you,
And loved the sorrows of your changing
    face.

*W. B. Yeats*

*T*o love oneself is the beginning of a lifelong romance.

*Oscar Wilde*

*T*ime is
Too slow for those who Wait,
Too swift for those who Fear,
Too long for those who Grieve;
Too short for those who Rejoice;
But for those who Love,
Time is Eternity.

*Henry Van Dyke*

*T*he holiest of all holidays are those
Kept by ourselves in silence and apart;
The secret anniversaries of the heart.

*Henry Wadsworth Longfellow*

*L*ove is like playing the piano. First you must learn to play by the rules. Then you must learn to play from the heart.

*Author Unknown*

*L*ove imperfectly. Be a love idiot. . . . Spill things. Tell secrets. Let yourself forget and love ideal or comparison. Be misshapen. Wake up laughing and cry frequently for no reason. Perfection in love is a narrow and suffocating path.

*Sark*

*T*he course of true anything never does run smooth.

*Samuel Butler*

# Success and
# Failure

$\mathcal{T}$here are two kinds of success. One is the very rare kind that comes to the man who has the power to do what no one else has the power to do. That is genius. But the average man who wins what we call success is not a genius. He is a man who has merely the ordinary qualities that he shares with his fellows, but who has developed those ordinary qualities to a more than ordinary degree.

*Theodore Roosevelt*

*A*lways demanding the best of oneself, living with honor, devoting one's talents and gifts to the benefits of others—these are the measures of success that endure when material things have passed away.

*Gerald R. Ford*

*T*he wealthy man is the man who is much, not the one who has much.

*Karl Marx*

*O*bstacles don't have to stop you.  If you run into a wall, don't turn around and give up.  Figure out how to climb it, go through it, or work around it.

*Michael Jordan*

One hundred percent of the shots you don't take don't go in.

*Wayne Gretzky*

*W*hen you come to the end of your rope, tie a knot and hang on.

*Franklin D. Roosevelt*

$\mathcal{T}$o laugh often and much; to win the respect of intelligent people and the affection of children; to earn the appreciation of honest critics and endure the betrayal of false friends; to appreciate beauty; to find the best in others; to leave the world a bit better, whether by a healthy child, a garden patch or a redeemed social condition; to know even one life has breathed easier because you have lived. This is to have succeeded.

*Ralph Waldo Emerson*

*F*all seven times, stand up eight.

*Japanese Proverb*